PEGASUS ENCYCLOPEDIA LIBRARY

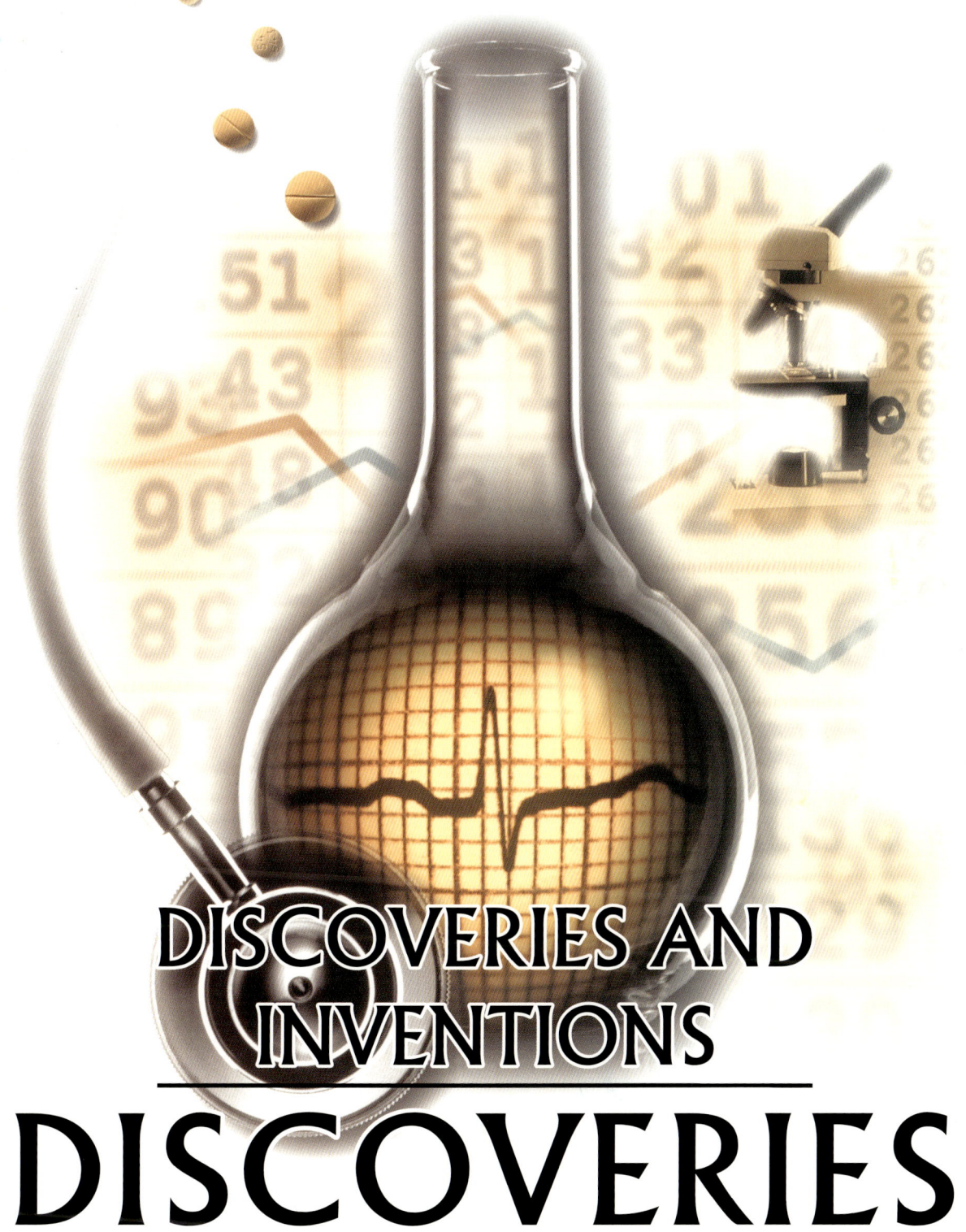

DISCOVERIES AND INVENTIONS
DISCOVERIES

Edited by: Anil Kumar Tomar, Pallabi B. Tomar
Managing editor: Tapasi De
Designed by: Vijesh Chahal, Anil Kumar, Rohit Kumar
Illustrated by: Suman S. Roy, Tanoy Choudhury
Colouring done by: Vinay Kumar, Sonu, Kiran Kumari & Pradeep Kumar

CONTENTS

What do we mean by a discovery? 3
The universe and planets 4
Blood circulation 5
The cell 6
Fire 8
Newton's Laws of Motion 9
Photosynthesis 11
Oxygen 12
Atomic Theory 13
The Saturn's Ring 14
Anaesthesia 15
Darwin's theory of evolution 16
Boyle's law of ideal gas 17
Rainbow—dispersion of light 18
Law of conservation of mass 19
Subatomic particles 20
The Nucleus 22
The Neutron 23
Vitamins 24
Fossils of dinosaurs 25
Radioactive Dating 26
Blood Transfusion 27
Penicillin 28
X-rays 29
Human Immunodeficiency Virus (HIV) 30
Test Your Memory 31
Index 32

What do we mean by a discovery?

Discoveries and inventions are used most of the times as synonyms but they are two different terms. A discovery refers to something which already exists, but which has been found by someone for the first time. An invention is something a man has produced quite new and which did not exist before.

For example, the blood circulation system in the human body existed since the existence of humans and it was discovered by William Harvey. This system could not be invented because it already existed.

Barometer was invented by Evangelista Torricelli to measure the atmospheric pressure. Barometer could not be discovered as it did not exist in the nature.

This book highlights some of the greatest discoveries of the world.

DISCOVERIES

The universe and planets

Everything that exists is the part of the universe. The galaxies are the biggest components of the universe each consisting of billions of stars. Each star has its solar system in which planets revolve around it. Our solar system, which consists of Earth and eight other planets revolving around the sun in an elliptical path, is embedded in Milky Way galaxy. The big bang theory explains the origin of universe and the way it is expanding. According to this theory, the universe is formed by expansion of an extremely dense and hot state and is continuously expanding.

Nicolaus Copernicus in 1543 ruled out all the previous assumptions about Earth, sun and stars. He placed the sun at the centre of the solar system and said

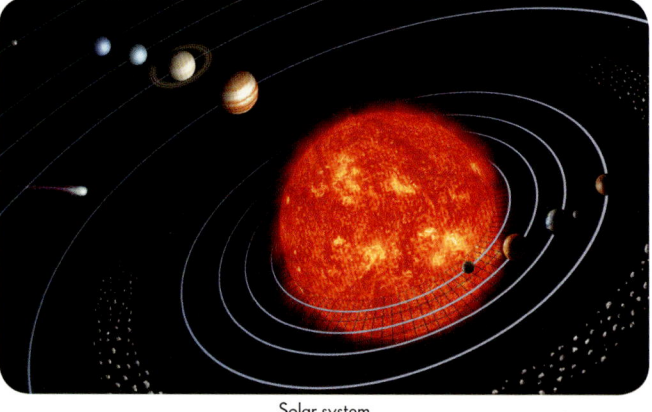
Solar system

Earth is not static but it moves around the sun. In early 17th century, Galileo Galilei discovered that Jupiter also has moons. Edwin Hubble (1924-1929) discovered for the first time that the universe is expanding. He also proved this by his experimental calculations and found that the galaxies which are farther from our galaxy are moving away with faster speed.

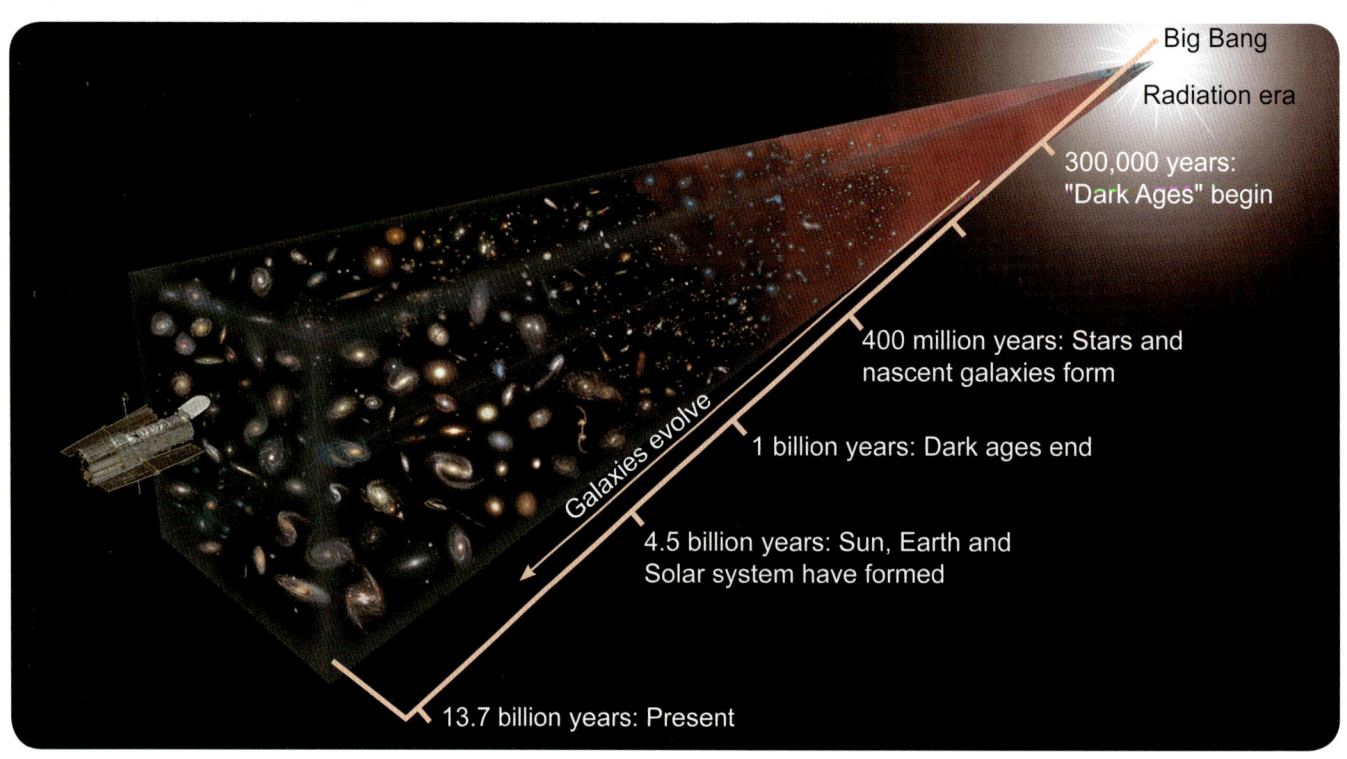
Big bang

Blood circulation

William Harvey, an English physician and anatomist discovered the circulation of the blood in 1628. He published his findings in *'Exercitatio Anatomica de Motu Cordis et Sanguinis in Animalibus'* (Anatomical Essay on the Motion of the Heart and Blood in Animals). This finding marks the beginning of modern physiology. During his experiments, Harvey observed that blood entered the right side of the heart and it was forced into the lungs before returning to the left side of the heart. From left heart, blood was pumped through the aorta into the arteries around the body. The detailed analysis made him realize that the amount of blood flowing through this system was too much for the liver to produce. Thus, he deduced that there is a blood circulation system and heart plays an important role to circulate blood through the system. Though he didn't observe blood capillaries as there was no microscope but he proposed the existence of tiny vessels that linked the arteries to the veins.

William Harvey

The cell

The cell, basic building block of all forms of life is the smallest unit which can be biologically defined as being alive. It was discovered in 1665 by an English scientist Robert Hooke. He was examining a dried thin section of a cork under a light microscope and discovered empty spaces contained by walls. He termed them pores or cells and was later credited for discovering the building blocks of all life. He recorded all his observations of small bodies visualized under his microscope into **Micrographia**. Robert Hooke described the cells as containers for the noble plant juices of the living cork tree. He also believed that cells existed only in plants since these structures were observed only in plant materials.

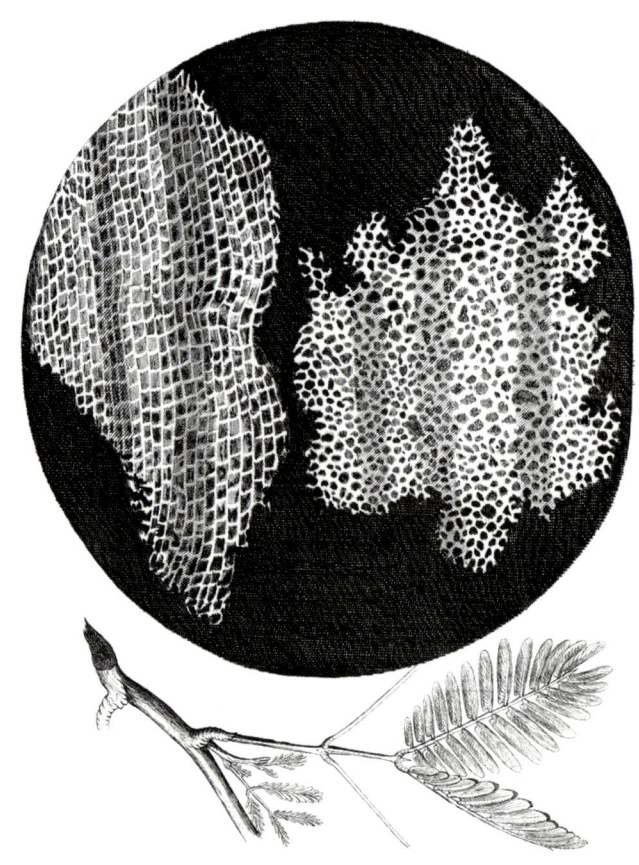

Robert Hooke

The cell Nucleus

For more than 100 years, it was believed that the cells could not further be subdivided. In 1831, an eminent Scottish botanist Robert Brown identified an opaque spot within the cells while he was observing the epidermis of a collection of orchids with his microscope. He used the term areola to describe them. He also observed this spot during the early stage of pollen formation. This made him conclude that this spot is key components of all cells and termed it as **nucleus**.

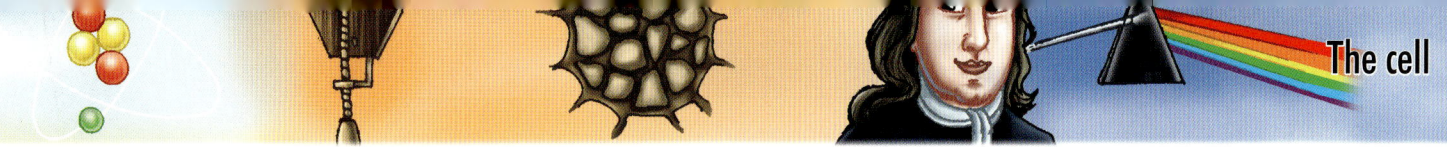

The cell

The cell theory

Various observations later revealed that cell is the basic building block of all living organisms and the cell theory came into existence. The cell theory was proposed by the German Scientists Jacob Schleiden and Theodore Schwann for the first time in 1838 and formalized by Rudolf Virchow in 1858.

The modern cell theory states that:

1. The cell is the basic structural and functional unit of life. All living organisms are composed of cells whether unicellular or multicellular.

2. All cells arise from preexisting cells. Each cell contains genetic material that is passed down during this process.

3. All basic chemical and physiological functions take place inside cells and activities of cells depend on the activities of sub cellular structures within the cell.

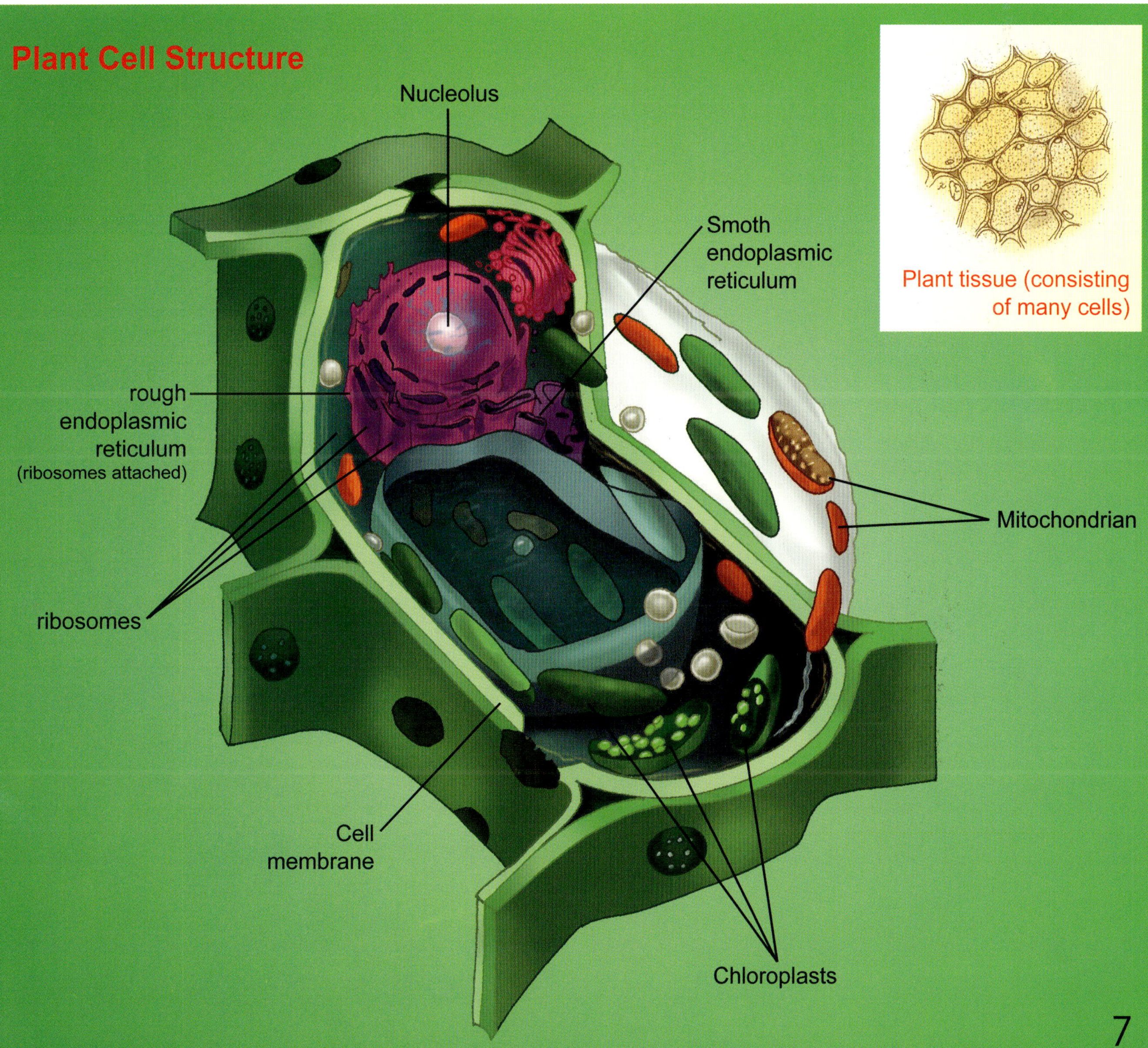

Plant Cell Structure

Plant tissue (consisting of many cells)

DISCOVERIES

Fire

Fire was undoubtedly one of our earliest gifts from nature. Human beings have known how to make and control fire since very ancient times. We do have evidence of hearths in caves dating back to almost a hundred thousand years ago in the dwellings of the Neanderthal Man. How this was first accomplished is shrouded in mystery, as indeed are so many other details pertaining to practically every initial giant step in human history. The creation of fire could well have been a chance discovery. Early humans were certainly familiar with the heat of the sun. They must have observed lightning flashes. A powerful lightning could have set a tree or a forest ablaze or a dry leaf or twig may have caught fire in the open, on a hot summer day. A human being may have generated sparks quite accidentally by aimless rubbing or scratching stones. With the discovery of ways of making of fire, men started cooking and this led to the human civilization.

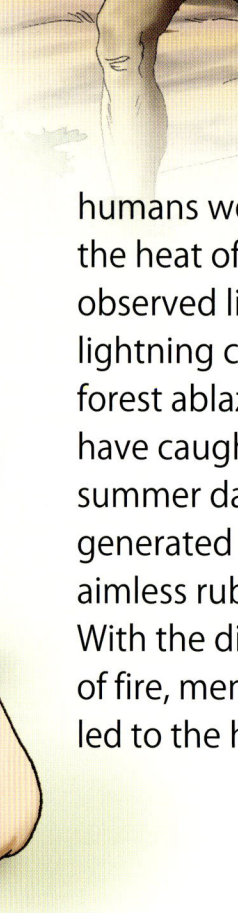
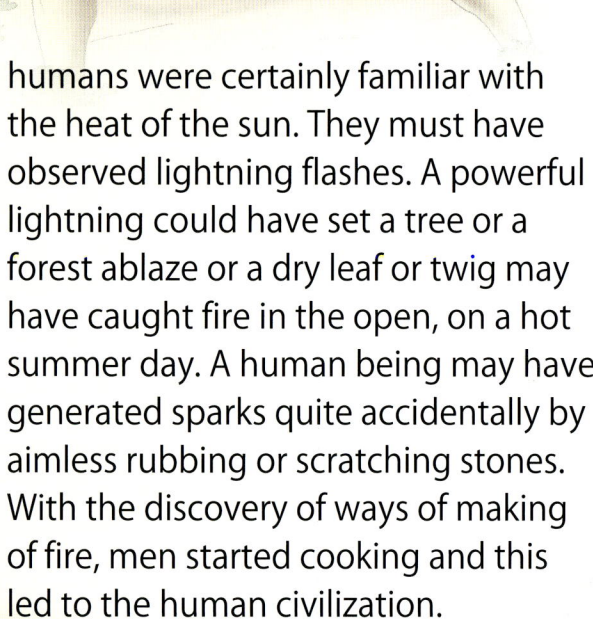

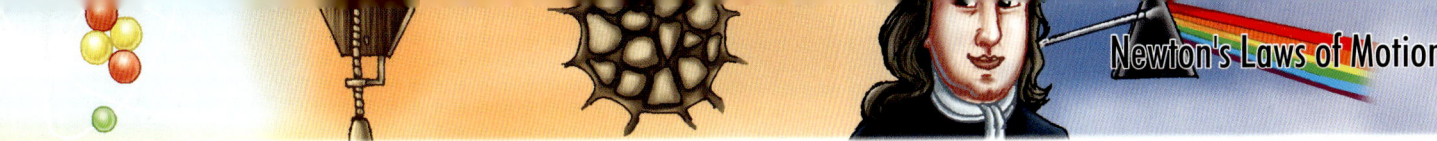

Newton's Laws of Motion

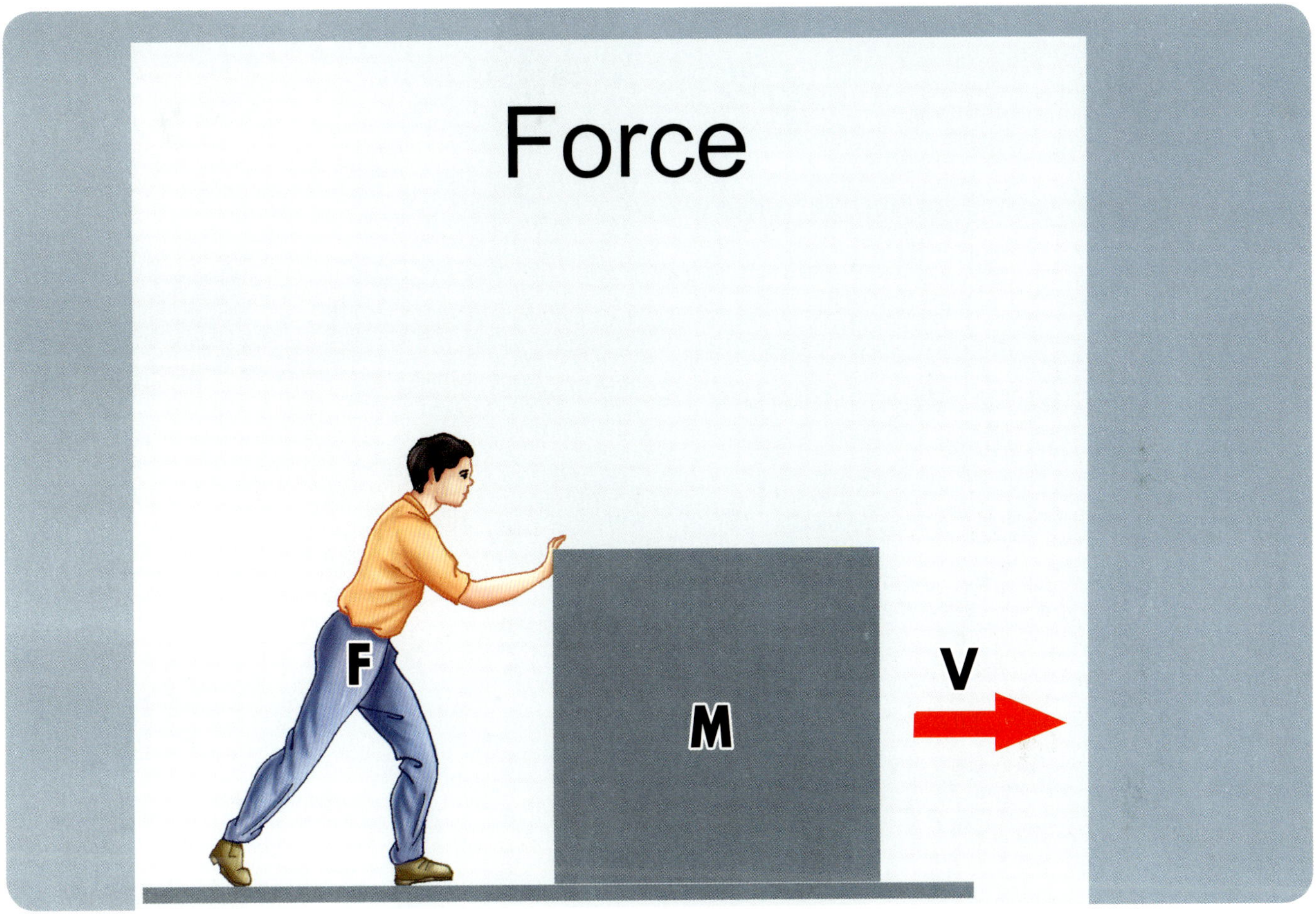

Isaac Newton was one of the greatest scientists of all the times in human history. He was an English physicist, mathematician, astronomer and philosopher. In 1687, he formulated three laws to describe the movement of objects which are the foundation of classical mechanics. The first, second and third laws are commonly known as **law of inertia**, **law of force** and **law of reciprocal actions** respectively.

Law of inertia: All bodies tend to remain at rest or to maintain a constant direction and speed, until some external force is not applied.

Law of force: If some external force is applied to a body, it produces acceleration in the direction of the applied force. The product of the acceleration and the mass of the object is equal to the force applied.

Law of reciprocal actions: For every action there is an equal and opposite reaction.

DISCOVERIES

Newton published **Philosophiae Naturalis Principia Mathematica (or Principia)** in 1687. This book explains Newton's three laws of motion and Universal law of gravitation.

The universal law of gravitation states that every particle of matter in the universe attracts every other particle with a force. This force acts along the line joining their centres and is directly proportional to the product of their masses and inversely proportional to the square of the distance between them.

Isaac Newton

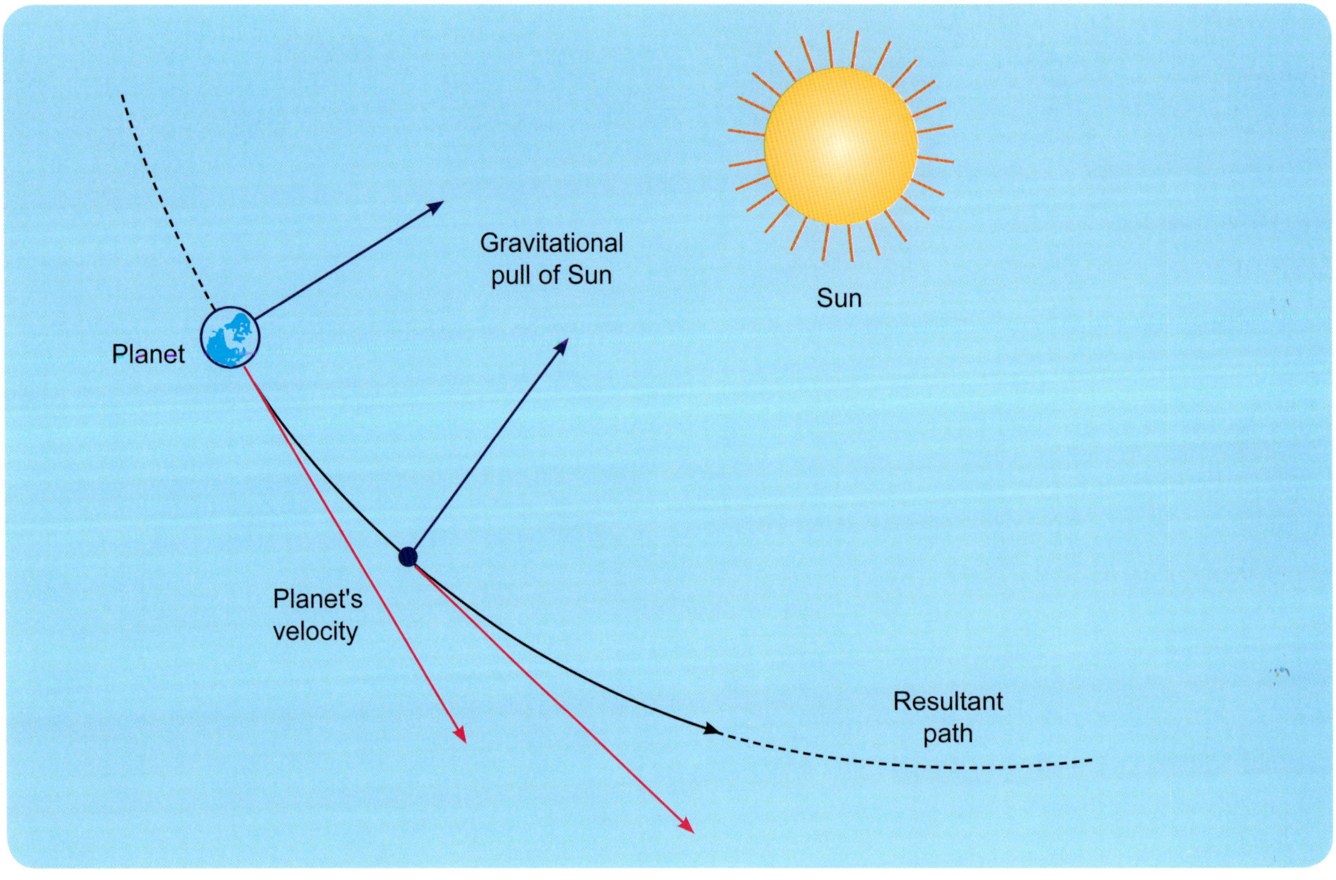

Photosynthesis

Plants, algae and some bacteria convert the light energy of the sun into the chemical energy through the process known as photosynthesis. The plants use captured sunlight to convert water and carbon dioxide into sugars like glucose. The process occurs in the chloroplasts and uses the green pigment of plants, chlorophyll. Thus, the basic ingredients of photosynthesis are carbon dioxide, water, chlorophyll and sunlight. The ancient Greek philosophers believed that plants obtained all of their nutrients from the soil. In the 17th century, Jan Baptista van Helmont, a Dutch physician and chemist performed experiments by growing a willow tree and concluded that the tree gained the weight from the water he added to the soil. Though he did not understand the process and its gradients but his experiments advanced the understanding of photosynthesis.

Julius Mayer

In 1771, Joseph Priestley implicated the role of atmospheric gases in plant growth. Jan Ingenhousz, a Dutch physician discovered that plants react to sunlight differently than shade. Through a series of experiments, he demonstrated that green parts of plants cleaned the air only when placed in strong light. In 1796, he also suggested that this process of photosynthesis causes carbon dioxide to split into carbon and oxygen and oxygen is released as a gas.

In 1804, the Swiss scientists, Nicholas Theodore de Saussure carefully measured the amounts of carbon dioxide and water that were given to the plant. He showed that the carbon in the plants came from carbon dioxide and the hydrogen from water. Finally in 1844, a German scientist, Julius Mayer, showed that the energy of sunlight is captured in photosynthesis.

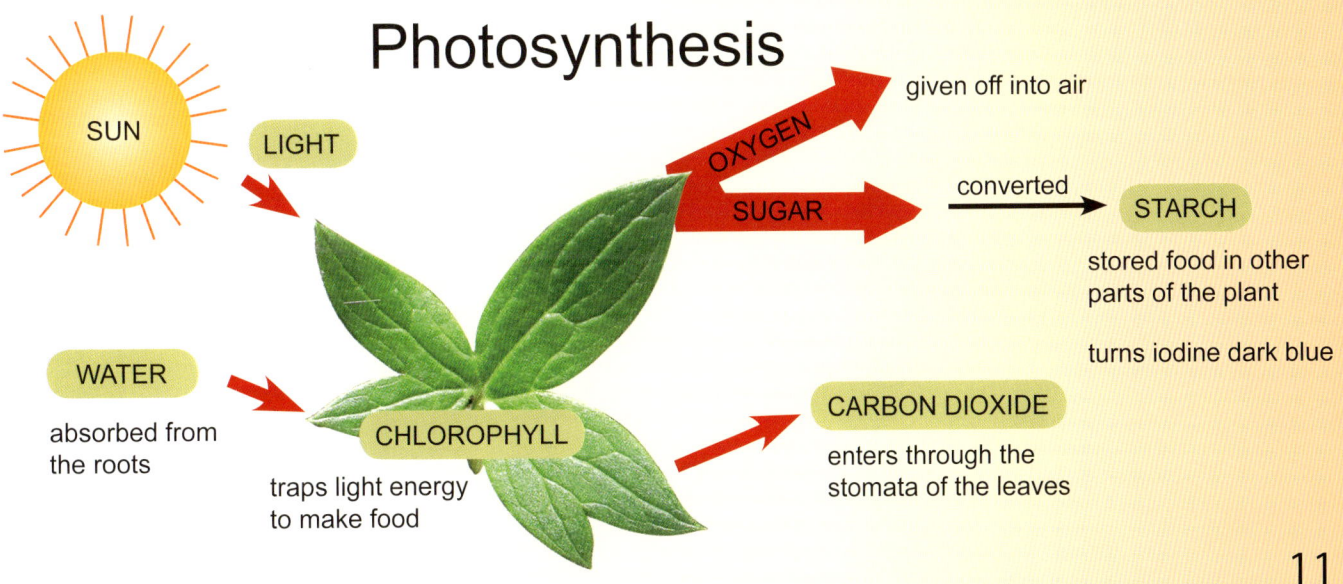

DISCOVERIES

Oxygen

Life on Earth cannot be imagined without oxygen. Animals and plants require it for respiration and to survive. It is tasteless, colourless and odourless gaseous element. It is the third most abundant element of the universe. It constitutes almost 21 per cent of the Earth's atmosphere and half of the Earth's crust. Oxygen is commonly used in oxidizers, rocket propulsion, medicines, welding, sensors, oxygen masks and concentrators.

Joseph Priestley

British chemist Joseph Priestley and the Swedish chemist Carl Wilhelm Scheele are credited for the discovery of oxygen by isolating oxygen in the gaseous state. Scheele was the first scientist who discovered oxygen in 1771 but it was Priestley who discovered oxygen in 1774 and proved that oxygen was essential to combustion and respiration. He published his findings in the same year and called the new gas 'dephlogisticated air'. The carbonated water, hydrochloric acid, nitrous oxide (commonly known as laughing gas), carbon monoxide and sulphur dioxide were also discovered by him. The name 'oxygen' was coined by a French chemist, Antoine Lavoisier in 1775. He was the first scientist who recognized oxygen as an element, characterized it and described its role in combustion.

Atomic Theory

Atomic theory is one of the greatest scientific discoveries of the 19th Century which marks the beginning of modern chemistry. A British school teacher, John Dalton, formulated this theory in the year 1803. For the first time in history, he recognized the difference between atom and compounds. This theory is based on his experiments and laws of chemical combinations.

John Dalton

Main postulates of Dalton's atomic theory are:

1) All matter is made of indivisible and indestructible particles called atoms.

2) All atoms of the same element are identical in mass and properties but they differ from the atoms of other elements.

3) Compounds are formed by a combination of atoms of two or more elements in a fixed whole number ratio.

4) Atoms are the smallest unit of matter and a chemical reaction is a rearrangement of atoms.

Though this theory many drawbacks and its assumptions were proved wrong but it enabled us to explain the laws of chemical combination.

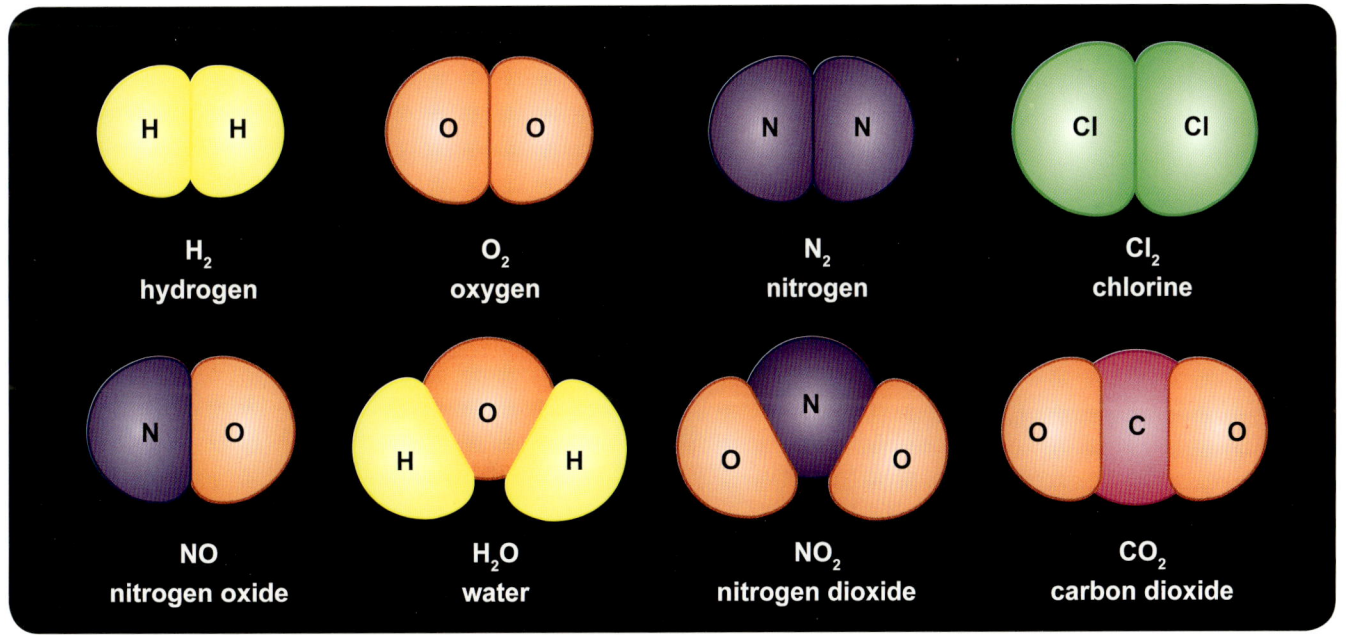

The Saturn's Ring

In 1610, Galileo Galilei observed a bright star flanked by two dimmer ones with his primitive telescope. He was amazed with the fact that the star he observed was not a single star, but three together, which almost touched each other. What he had discovered was a planet that was to become one of the wonders of the solar system. This planet was later named 'Saturn'. Saturn's beauty comes from its magnificent rings. Galileo described them as 'handles' or large moons on either side of the planet. Galileo's discovery of Saturn commenced the scientific process of unravelling the mysteries of Saturn's extensive ring system. But even after 400 years the mysteries have not been all solved. In 1655, Christann Huyges proposed that Saturn was surrounded by a solid ring. He described this ring as a thin and flat ring which nowhere touched the Saturn and was inclined to the ecliptic. As time went on, more and more observations were made and theories proposed. According to the modern prominent theories, the ring is made out of small particles rather than being solid.

Anaesthesia

Anaesthesia is used to produce a condition in the body of having sensation blocked or temporarily taken away. This allows patients to undergo surgery and other procedures without the distress and pain they would otherwise experience. The discovery of surgical anaesthesia in the early 1840s represented a unique American contribution to medicine. The word anaesthesia was coined by Oliver Wendell Holmes, Sr. in 1846.

Before the mid 1800's a person undergoing surgery was in for a terrifying time. In those pre-anaesthetic days, there was nothing to dull the pain but whiskey. Attempts to dull the pain of patients led to the use of marijuana, opium and hashish in China and India. In the 1840s ether became popular for recreational use. One day an American physician by the name of Crawford W. Long noted that people under the influence of ether felt no pain. He immediately realised the potential to relieve the pain of surgery.

The first operation using ether as an anaesthetic took place on March 30th, 1842. Later, nitrous oxide (laughing gas) and Chloroform were also used as anaesthesia. Advancements were made that allowed a patient to remain awake while a specific part of their body was made anaesthetic.

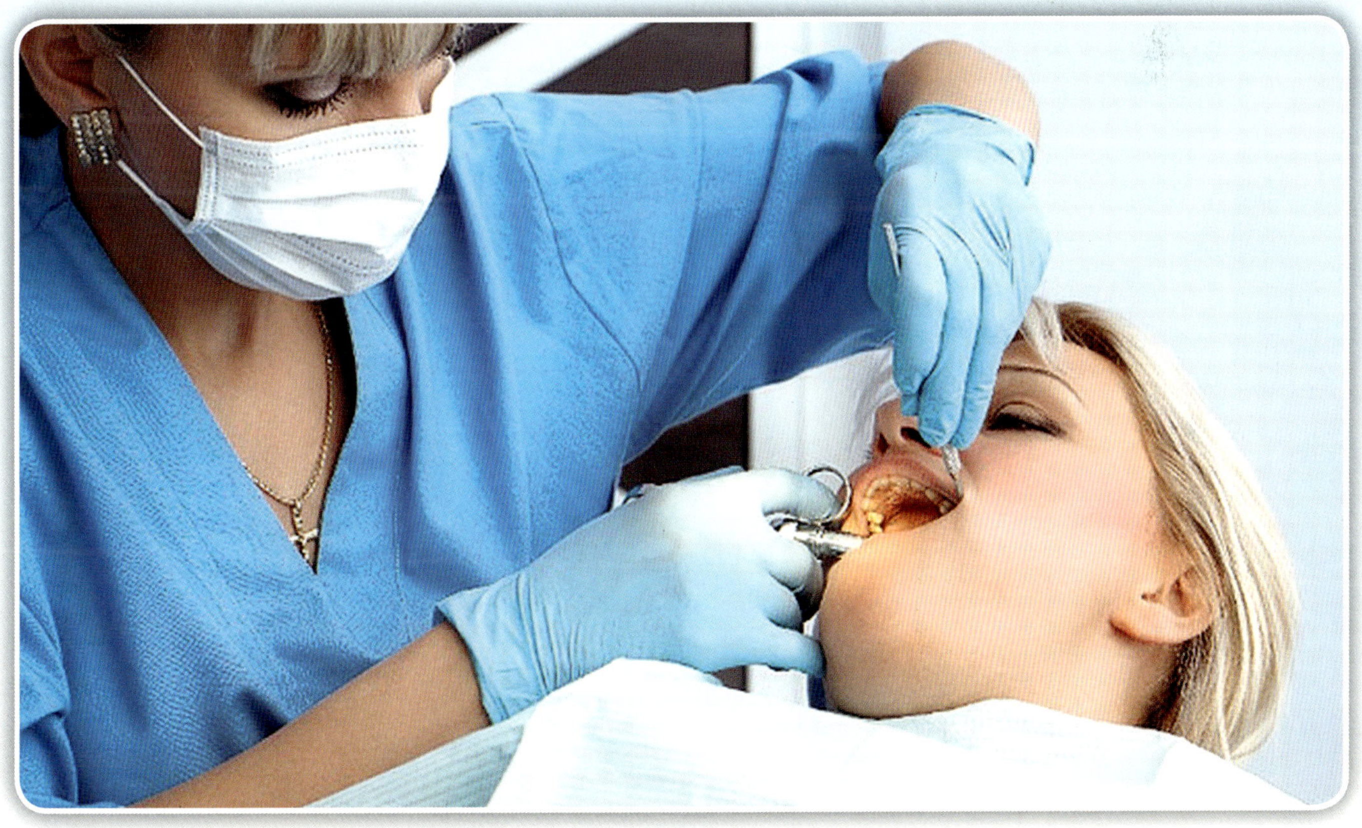

Darwin's theory of evolution

The theory of evolution is one of the greatest scientific revolutions of human history. It drastically changed our perception of the world and of our place in it. Charles Darwin put forth a coherent theory of evolution and gathered a great body of evidence in support of this theory. Darwin's Theory of Evolution is the widely held notion that all life is related and has descended from a common ancestor; that is, the birds and the bananas, the fishes and the flowers, all have common ancestors. According to Darwin's theory, the development of life from non-life and stresses a purely naturalistic 'descent with modification'. That is, complex creatures evolve from more simplistic ancestors naturally over time. He also suggested that random genetic mutations occur within an organism's genetic code and the beneficial mutations are preserved because they aid survival. This process is known as 'natural selection'. These beneficial mutations are passed on to the next generation. Over the time, beneficial mutations accumulate and the result is an entirely different organism. The new organism maybe a variation of the original or an entirely different creature.

Charles Darwin

Boyle's law of ideal gas

Robert Boyle (1627-1691) was an Irish-born philosopher who did research and investigation in physics, chemistry and theology. Boyle is known as the founder of modern chemistry because he believed in the intrinsic value of chemistry, developed the rigorous experimental scientific method and defined the element. In 1962, he proved his law for both great and small pressures and discovered a law of ideal gases. This law states that if we keep the temperature constant, pressure is inversely proportional to the volume. In simple words, pressure increases

DISCOVERIES

Rainbow—dispersion of light

Dispersion is the separation of a beam of light into its constituent colours. This takes place when a light beam passes through a dispersive medium. The sunlight is often called white light as it constitutes all the visible colours. It disperses into a spectra of seven colours when passes through a glass prism. In 1666, Sir Isaac Newton used a prism to disperse white light and discovered the constituent colours of white light. When light passes through a prism, it passes through two interfaces between glass and air. The light bends towards the normal when it enters the prism and away from the normal when it exits. As the two interfaces are at an angle, the dispersion is very easy to observe. The seven colours of white light are violet, indigo, blue, green, yellow, orange and red.

A well-known example of dispersion is the formation of a rainbow. A rainbow is formed when white light is dispersed through raindrops. Tiny droplets of water refract the white light from the sun and create a spectrum of colours similar to what happens in a prism. Since the droplets are spheres, the light is reflected internally in the droplets and the spectrum or rainbow returns toward the direction of the light. That is why the sun is always behind us when we see a rainbow.

Law of conservation of mass

The law of conservation of mass states that the mass of substances in a closed system will remain constant, no matter what processes are acting inside the system. This universally accepted law explains that the matter may change from one form to another but it can neither be created nor destroyed. The mass of the reactants must always equal the mass of the products. This law was first formulated by Antoine Lavoisier in 1789. Some evidences also highlight that Mikhail Lomonosov, in 1748, had also expressed similar ideas. Thus, this law is commonly known as the Lomonosov-Lavoisier law. This law was the key to making chemistry into a real science which marked the beginning of modern chemistry. After this, the ideas of chemical elements, process of fire and oxidation and many other basic chemical principles could be better understood. In most situations the law of conservation of mass can be assumed valid. This law works fine for anything except for the matter that is approaching the speed of light. At high speeds, mass begins transforming to energy. Due to this reason, we now have the Law of Conservation of Mass and Energy.

Antoine Lavoisier

Subatomic particles

Atoms are made up of three particles- electron, proton and neutron. Hydrogen atom is an exception as it does not have any neutron. The nucleus of an atom makes up the most of an atom's mass and consists of protons and neutrons. The electrons are smaller particles and revolve around the nucleus. The protons and electrons have positive and negative charges respectively while the neutrons are electrically neutral. An atom has the same number of electrons and protons to make it electrically neutral.

The Electron

Dalton's atomic theory stated that atoms make up all matter in the universe and they were, by definition, indivisible. But even before the entire scientific community accepted the facts of this theory, scientists disapproved the fact that atoms are indivisible. They believed that atoms were made up of even smaller entities.

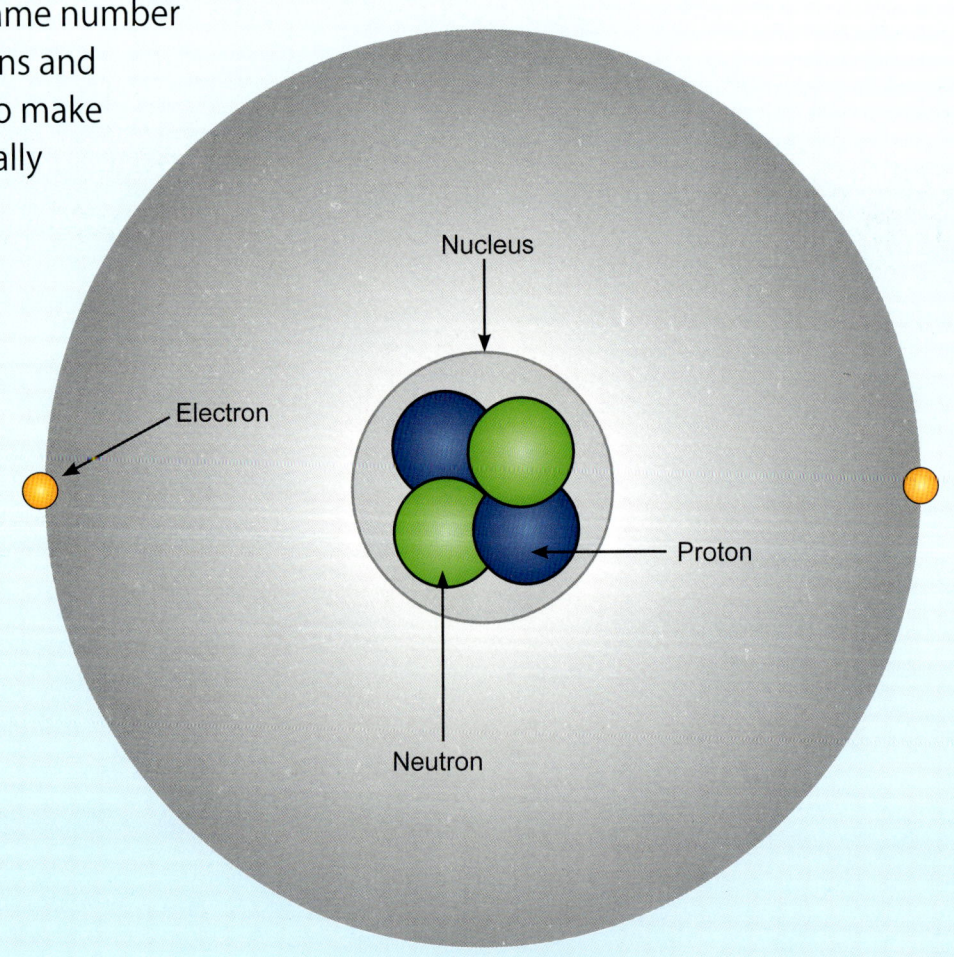

Subatomic particles

J.J. Thompson

In 1897, the British Physicist J.J. Thompson discovered the first subatomic particle – the electron while he was experimenting with a cathode ray tube at Cambridge University. He was working to find the constituent particles of cathode rays. In his experiment, he was able to bend the ray using a magnetic field and measured the direction in which the ray bent to determine both mass and charge. Based on his experiments, he proposed that something smaller than an atom existed in the form of tiny negatively charged particles.

Now it is well established that electrons are fundamental aspects of the atomic structure and they provide necessary charge to neutralize the atomic structure. The molecules are formed by combinations of atoms and these combinations are only possible by the bonds formed by electrons. An electron has a mass of 9.11×10^{-31} kg and a charge equal to 1.602×10^{-19} coulomb.

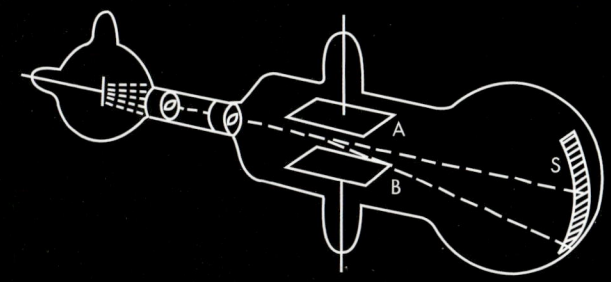

The Nucleus

The positively charged nucleus of an atom was discovered by New Zealand physicist Ernest Rutherford in 1909 during the Gold Foil experiment. This experiment was performed by Hans Geiger and Ernest Marsden at the University of Manchester under his guidance. In this experiment, positively charged alpha particles were fired at a high velocity into a very thin sheet of gold foil. The trajectories of these particles after passing through the foil were then detected and analyzed. Most of the alpha particles travelled straight through the foil with little or no deviation and a small fraction rebounded, ending up on the same side of the foil as the incoming beam. Based on these observations, Rutherford proposed new atomic model which states that

Ernest Rutherford

negatively charged electrons orbited around a positively charged and incredibly dense central 'nucleus'. Through a series of experiments in 1918, Rutherford discovered that the positively charged particles were known as the proton. He also deduced that they are subatomic particles and the atom is divisible.

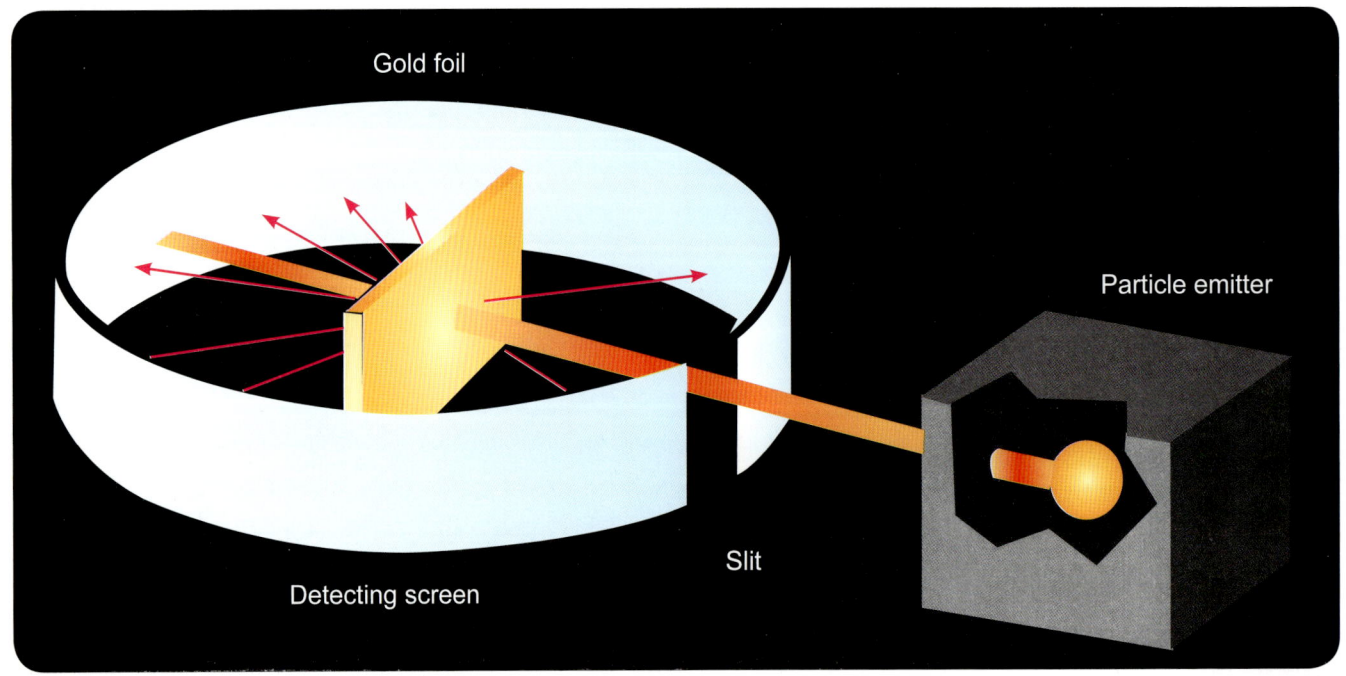

The Neutron

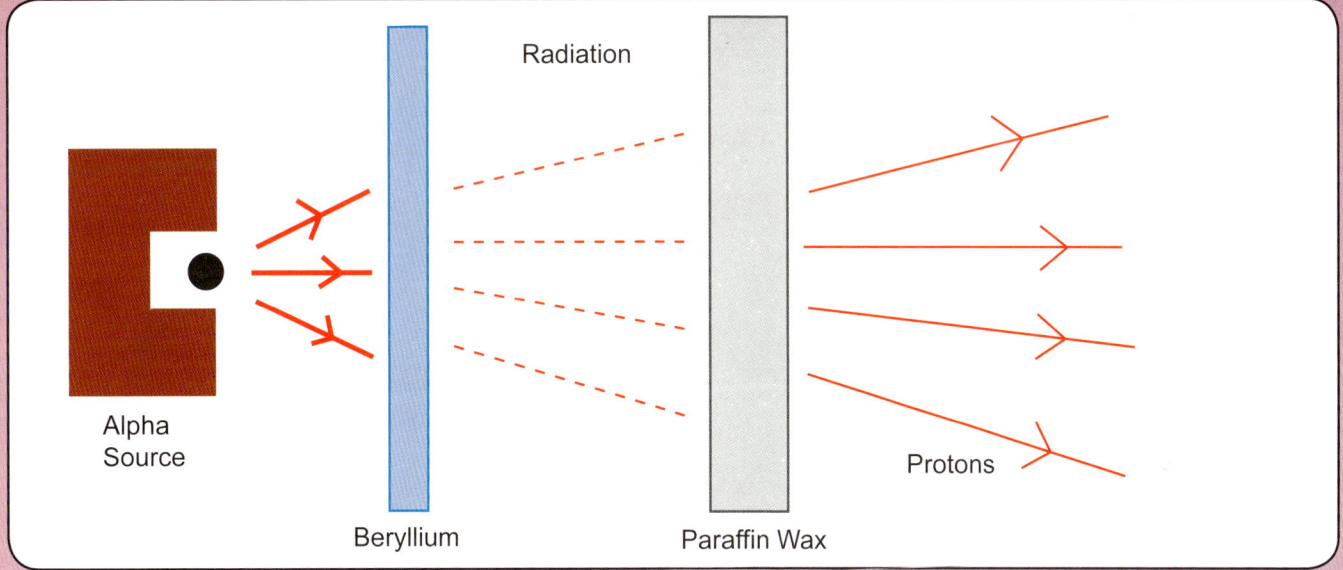

The neutron was discovered by James Chadwick in 1932. He bombarded beryllium (Be) with alpha particles and allowed the radiation emitted by beryllium to incident on a paraffin wax. It was found that protons were scattered out from the paraffin wax. He analyzed the scattered data and proved that the radiation consisted of neutral particles of mass approximately equal to that of proton. These neutral particles were named neutrons. Sir Chadwick was awarded with Noble Prize of Physics for his findings in 1935.

This discovery marked the adoption of the Rutherford-Bohr model of the atom. The main assumptions of this model are:

1. The nucleus of an atom is made up of protons and neutrons which are bound together by strong nuclear forces.
2. Electrons orbit the nucleus in the fixed shells.
3. Electrons and protons carry equal but opposite charges. The number of electrons and protons is the same in a neutral atom.

James Chadwick

Vitamins

Vitamins are natural substances which are essential nutrients for humans. Deficiency of vitamins makes humans sick. To stay healthy, we need food rich in all type of vitamins as most of the vitamins (except vitamin D & K) cannot be synthesized by our body. In 1905, an English scientist William Fletcher while searching for the cause of disease Beriberi discovered that eating unpolished rice prevented Beriberi and eating polished rice did not. He suggested that there were some special factors or nutrients in the husk of the rice and if they were removed from food, disease is caused. In 1906, Sir Frederick Gowland Hopkins also discovered that some food factors were important to health. The term 'vitamine' was coined by Polish scientist Cashmir Funk in 1912 for these special nutritional parts of food. The name was later shortened to vitamin.

Fossils of dinosaurs

Dinosaurs are a diverse group of extinct animals that were the dominant terrestrial vertebrates for over 160 million years, from the late Triassic period until the end of the Cretaceous. A British fossil finder William Buckland discovered the first dinosaur fossil remains of our modern times. In 1819, Buckland discovered the Megalosaurus Bucklandii (Buckland's Giant Lizard) in England. It was given its name in 1824. Prior to this, Reverend Plot had found a huge femur bone as early as 1676 in England. It was thought to belong to a giant. Many anthropologists suggested that it might have belonged to a dinosaur. However, with the discovery of giant human skeletal remains ranging from 8 ft to 12 ft tall around the world in the last few hundred years, many believe the Plot femur may have belonged to a very tall human. In 1838, William Parker Foulke found the first complete dinosaur fossil in New Jersey, USA. Since Buckland's original discovery in 1819, hundreds of different dinosaur genera have been discovered so far.

Radioactive Dating

The age of Earth has been a topic of long debate throughout the scientific community. Bertram Boltwood, an American chemist, discovered the method to calculate the age of a rock in 1907 by measuring the rate of Uranium-238 radioactive decay. Boltwood proposed that the age of a rock containing Uranium-238 can be determined by measuring the remaining amount of uranium-238 and the relative amount of the decaying product lead-206. Using his method, he estimated the age of Earth to be 2.2 billion years.

Radioactive dating methods are based on the disintegration property of radioactive substances. These substances eventually decay during the course of time into the stable nuclides. If the rate of decay is known, we can determine the age of a specimen containing radioactive substance by estimating the relative proportions of the remaining radioactive substance and the product of its decay. Carbon-14, Uranium-235, Uranium-238 and Thorium-232 are some of the common radioactive substances with approximate half life of 5730 years, 700 million years, 4.5 billion years and 14 billion years respectively.

Blood transfusion

Blood transfusion can be life-saving and necessary in the cases of extreme blood loss due to trauma or can be used to replace blood lost during surgery. Blood transfusions may also be used to treat a severe anaemia or other blood diseases. People suffering from haemophilia or sickle-cell anaemia disease may require frequent blood transfusions. Blood transfusions, in early times, used whole blood, but modern strategy is to use only components of the blood. Knowledge of the different blood types is crucial for safe blood transfusions. The most accepted blood classification is ABO system according to which all humans have one of the following four blood groups – A, B, AB or O. In 1901, an Austrian biologist Karl Landsteiner and his group discovered blood groups and developed a system of classification. For his discovery he was awarded the Nobel Prize in Medicine in 1930. He is also credited for discovering blood antigens and antibodies, specific to the blood groups.

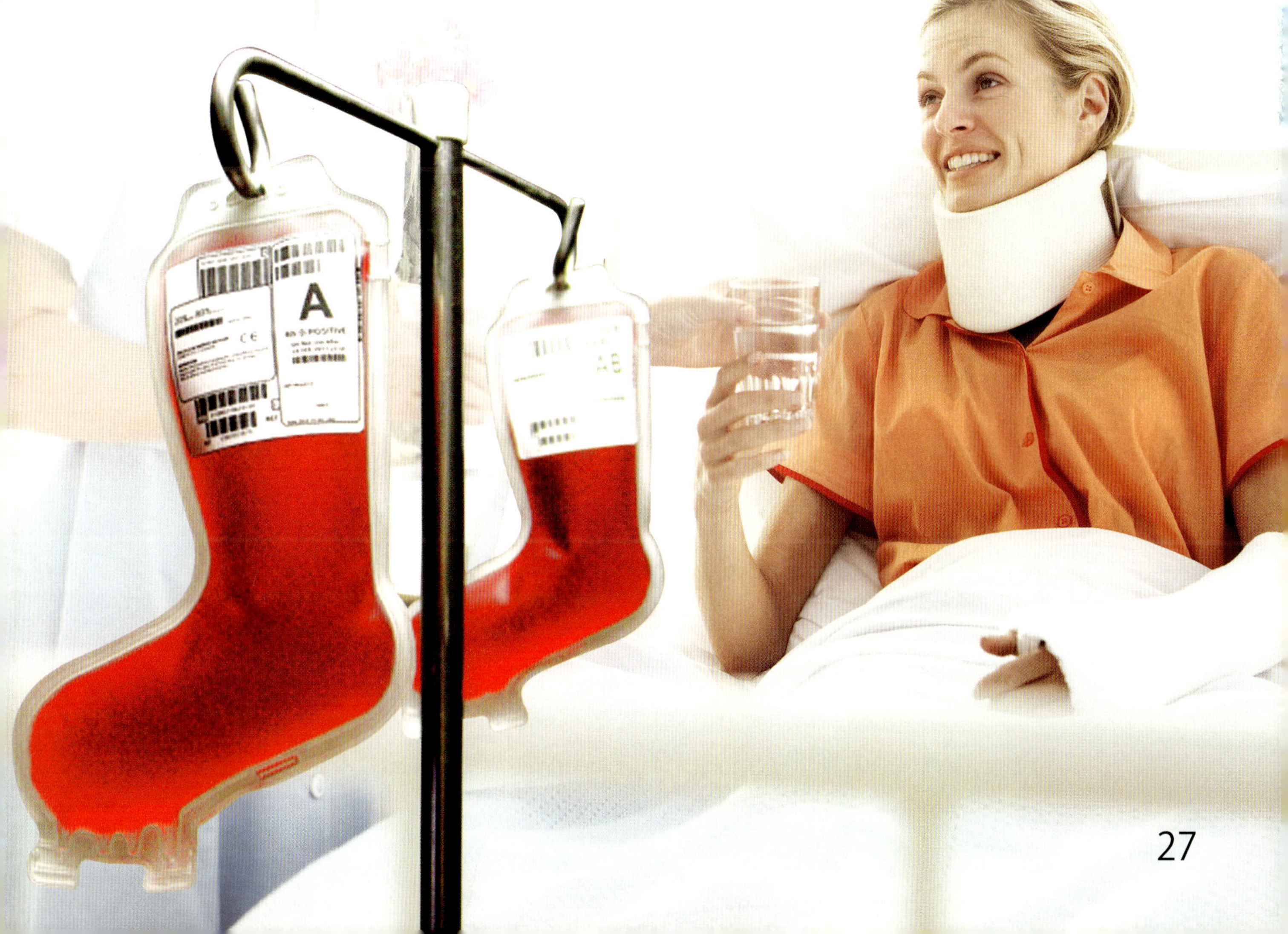

Penicillin

Alexander Fleming

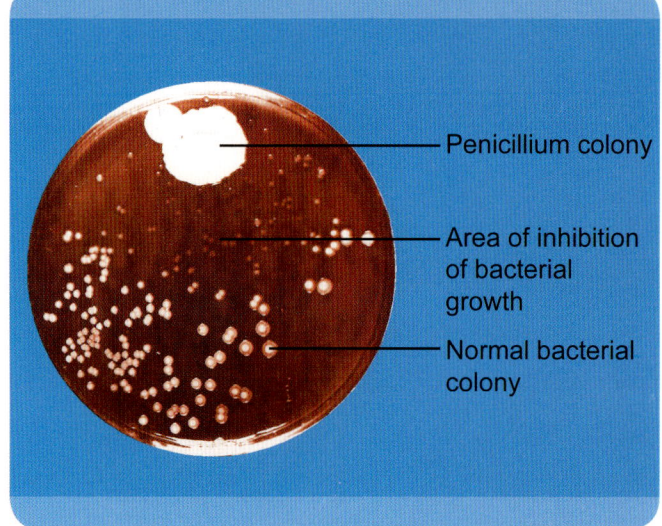

Penicillin was discovered accidentally by Dr. Alexander Fleming while working at St. Mary's Hospital in London. He was examining a culture of **Staphylococcus aureus**, a pathogenic bacterium when he noticed that it had been contaminated by a mold. He observed that species of the mold was inhibiting the bacterial growth. He took a sample of the mold and characterized it. He found that it belonged to penicillium family and could treat many types of harmful bacterial infections. Later, he named it penicillin and reported his findings in 1929. However, penicillin, the first antibiotic, was isolated by Howard Florey and Ernst Chain during the Second World War. This discovery revolutionized the medicinal research and recognized as the greatest advances in therapeutics. Fleming along with Florey and Chain received a Nobel Prize in 1945 for their discovery which led to the development of lifesaving antibiotics.

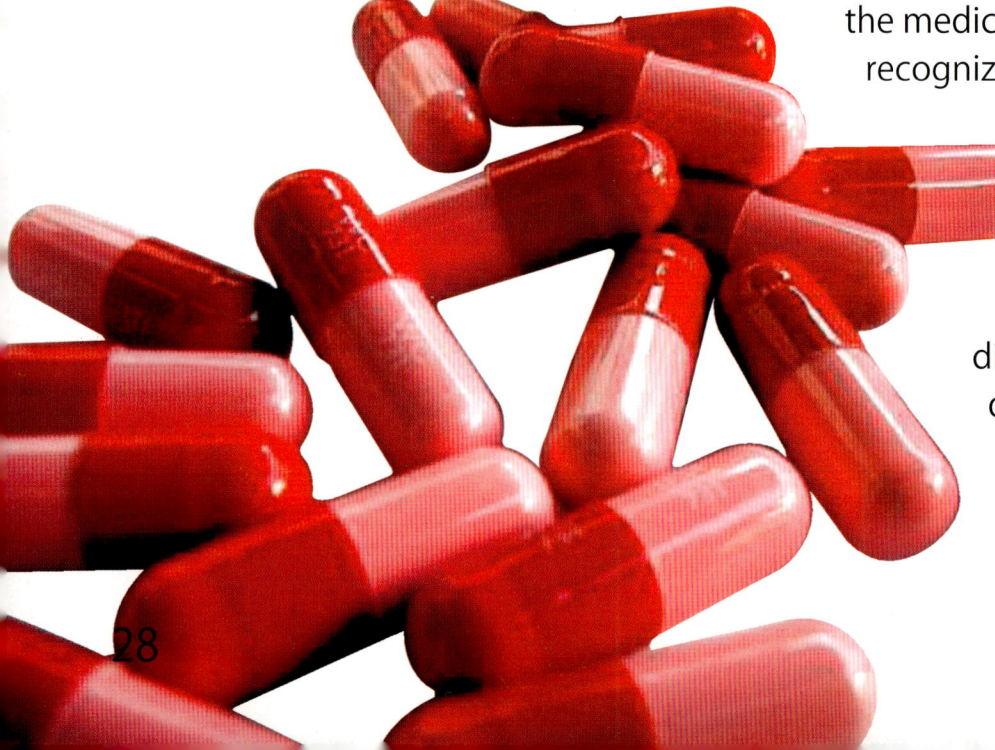

X-rays

Wilhelm Roentgen accidentally discovered X-rays when he was conducting experiments with the radiation from cathode rays. He noticed that the rays were able to penetrate opaque black paper wrapped around a cathode ray tube, causing a nearby table to glow with florescence. He also found that the new ray would pass through most substances casting shadows of solid objects on pieces of film. He named the new ray X-ray because in mathematics 'X' denotes the unknown quantity. The first image Roentgen took was an X-ray film of his wife Bertha's hand. The news of Roentgen's discovery spread quickly throughout the world. In early 1896, X-rays were being utilized clinically in the United States for capturing images of bone fractures and gunshot wounds. For this discovery, Roentgen was awarded with the first-ever Nobel Prize for physics in 1901.

Wilhelm Roentgen

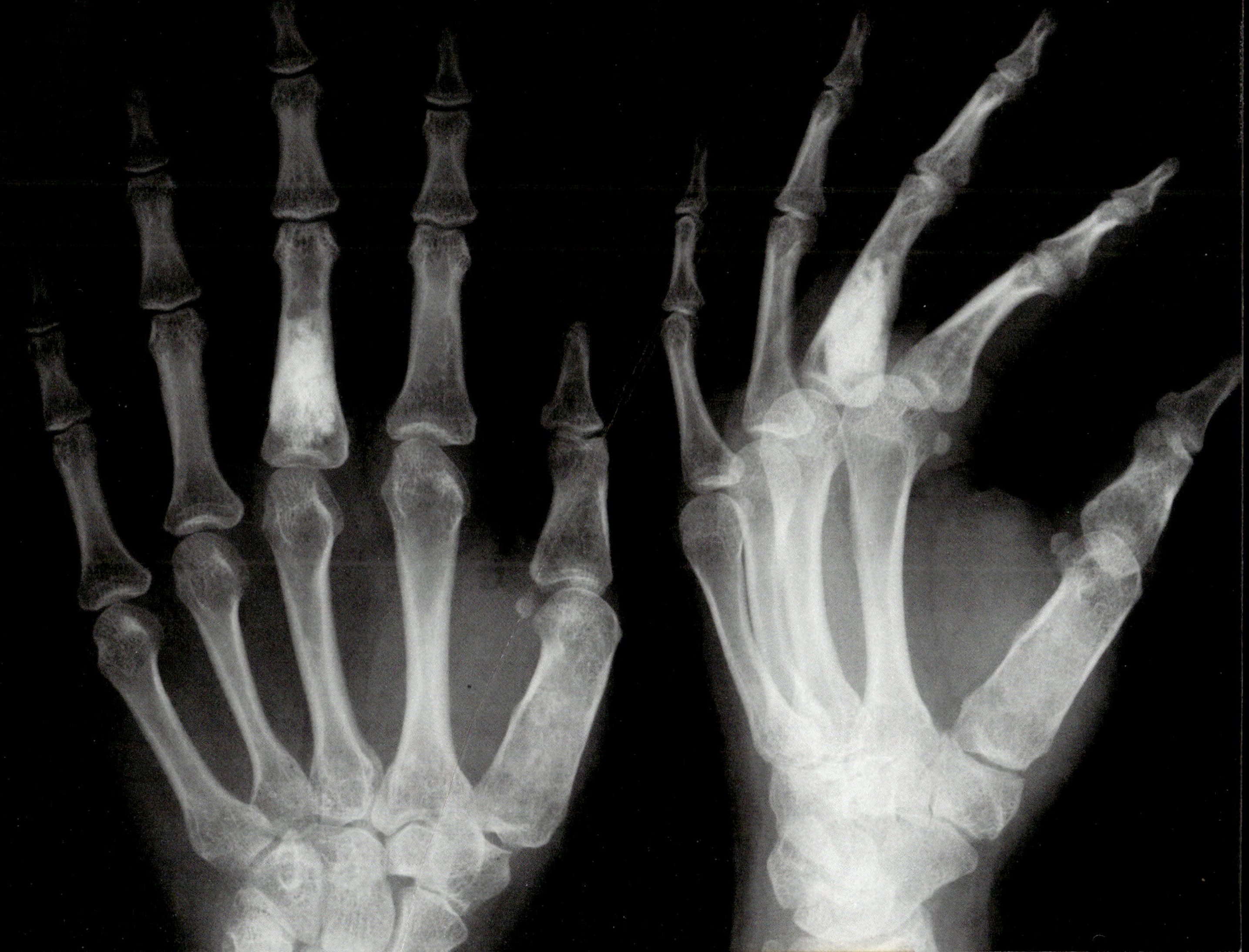

Human Immunodeficiency Virus (HIV)

Dr Montagnier and his colleagues discovered HIV as the cause **Human Immunodeficiency Virus**. Human Immunodeficiency Virus (HIV) is the causative agent of an infectious disease, **Acquired Immune Deficiency Syndrome** (AIDS). AIDS is a condition in humans in which the immune system begins to fail, leading to life-threatening opportunistic infections. Infection with HIV occurs by the transfer of blood, semen, vaginal fluid, pre-ejaculate or breast milk. Within these bodily fluids, HIV is present as both free virus particles and virus within infected immune cells. The four major routes of transmission are unsafe sex, contaminated needles, breast milk, and perinatal transmission (transmission from an infected mother to her baby at birth). AIDS was first recognized as a new disease in 1981, when a number of young men in New York and Los Angeles were diagnosed with symptoms not usually seen in individuals with healthy immune systems. This information was reported to the Centres for Disease Control and Prevention (CDC), the branch of the U.S. government that monitors and tries to control disease outbreaks.

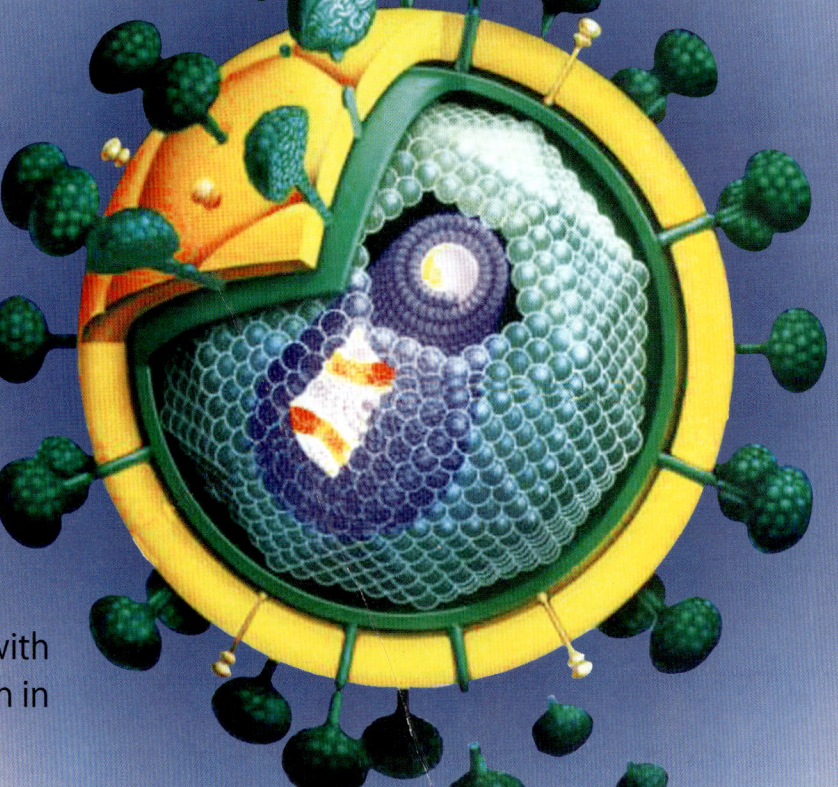

Test Your MEMORY

1. What is the difference between a discovery and an invention?
2. Who proposed the cell theory and what are the main postulates of this theory?
3. What is the big bang theory?
4. What is the Boyle's law of ideal gases?
5. What are the basic requirements of photosynthesis?
6. Explain Newton's laws of motion.
7. What is the universal law of gravitation?
8. Name the subatomic particles. Who discovered them?
9. Explain the law of conservation of mass.
10. What is anaesthesia used for?
11. What is HIV?
12. Describe the process of radioactive dating to find the age of a rock.

Index

A
Acquired Immune Deficiency Syndrome 30
anaesthesia 15
antibiotic 28

B
barometer 3
beriberi 24
big bang theory 4

C
cathode ray 21, 29
cells 6, 7, 30
chlorophyll 11
combustion 12

D
dinosaurs 25
discoveries 3, 13

E
Earth 4, 12, 26
electron 20, 21
Ernest Marsden 22
Ernest Rutherford 22

F
force 9, 10
Frederick Gowland Hopkins 24

G
galaxies 4
Galileo 4, 14
glucose 11

H
haemophilia 27
Hans Geiger 22
Human Immunodeficiency Virus 30

I
inertia 9
inventions 3

J
James Chadwick 23
J.J. Thompson 21

M
magnetic field 21
marijuana 15
mass 9, 13, 19, 20, 21, 23

N
Neanderthal Man 8
neutron 20, 23
Nicolaus Copernicus 4
nucleus 6, 20, 22, 23
nutrients 11, 24

O
opium 15
oxygen 11, 12

P
penicillin 28
photosynthesis 11
pressure 3, 17
prism 18
proton 20, 22, 23

R
radiation 23, 29
radioactive dating 26
respiration 12
Rutherford-Bohr model 23

S
Staphylococcus aureus 28

T
transmission 30

V
vitamins 24
volume 17

W
William Fletcher 24

X
X-rays 29